Canadian Symbols

Beavers

by Sabrina Crewe

CAPSTONE PRESS
a capstone imprint

Pebble Plus is published by Capstone Press,
1710 Roe Crest Drive, North Mankato, Minnesota 56003
www.capstonepub.com

Library of Congress Cataloging-in-Publication Data
Cataloging-in-publication information is on file with the Library of Congress.

ISBN 978–1-4914-7091-6 (library binding : alk. paper)
ISBN 978–1-4914-7097-8 (pbk. : alk. paper)
ISBN 978–1-4914-7109-8 (eBook PDF)

Developed and Produced by Discovery Books Limited
Paul Humphrey: project manager
Sabrina Crewe: editor
Ian Winton: designer

Photo Credits
BMJ/Shutterstock: cover; Pictureguy/Shutterstock: title page; Jody Ann/Shutterstock: 5; Jean-Pierre Lavoie/Shutterstock: 7; A. J. Gallant/Shutterstock: 9; Scott Karcich/Shutterstock: 9 (inset); Henrik Larsson/Shutterstock: 11; ValeStock/Shutterstock: 13 (top); Riekephotos/Shutterstock: 13 (bottom); Massimiliano Pieraccini/Shutterstock: 15; © Royal Canadian Mint. All rights reserved/Pete Spiro/Shutterstock: 17 (top); Boris15/Shutterstock: 17 (bottom); Mighty Sequoia Studio/Shutterstock: 19; Scouts Canada: 21 (both).

Note to Parents and Teachers
This book describes and illustrates beavers. The images support early readers in understanding text. The repetition of words and phrases helps early readers learn new words. This book also introduces early readers to subject-specific vocabulary words, which are defined in the Glossary section. Early readers may need assistance to read some words and to use the Table of Contents, Glossary, Read More, Internet Sites, and Index sections of the book.

Printed in China through World Print Ltd in 2014
007272WPS15

Table of Contents

A Symbol for Canada

A symbol is a picture or object
that stands for something
important. Symbols can stand
for ideas, beliefs, and countries.
The beaver has been a symbol
of Canada for a long time.

Beavers live all over Canada.

About Beavers

Beavers are Canada's biggest rodents. They spend a lot of time in the water. Their thick, oily fur keeps out water. Beavers use their large tails to steer.

A beaver steers with its tail.

Beavers have strong teeth to gnaw on tree trunks and branches. They use the wood to build dams across streams and rivers. The dams hold back water to make ponds.

This pond was formed when beavers built the dam across the stream.

This tree was gnawed by a beaver.

9

Beavers live in lodges in ponds. They make their lodges with mud and branches. The lodge entrances are underwater, but inside the nest is dry.

A beaver family lives inside this lodge.

Emblems and Symbols

Long ago, fur traders killed millions of beavers. They sold the beaver fur and made lots of money. The fur traders put four beavers on their emblem.

You can see the beavers on the fur traders' emblem.

PRO PELLE CUTEM

Fur traders sold bundles of beaver fur for making hats.

The beaver has been used on other emblems, too. It was used in Nova Scotia and Quebec. In 1975, the beaver became a symbol of Canada.

This beaver is on the Parliament Building in Ottawa.

You can see a beaver on our five-cent coin, the nickel. Several stamps have shown a beaver, too. The first Canadian stamp was the "Three-Penny Beaver." It was made in 1851.

A Canadian nickel

A "Three-Penny Beaver" postage stamp

Busy as a Beaver

Beavers work hard, and they always seem busy. That is why we say someone is "busy as a beaver." For some First Peoples, the beaver stands for hard work. It is also a clan symbol.

This totem pole shows a beaver holding its tail.

Beaver Scouts are girls and boys who are 5, 6, or 7 years old. The Beaver Scouts' law says: A Beaver has fun, works hard, and helps family and friends.

Beaver Scouts like to share and play together.

Glossary

clan—a connected group of people, like a family but larger

dam—a barrier that stops water

emblem—a badge or shield that shows a symbol

fur trader—a person who hunts animals and sells their fur

gnaw—chew something until it wears away

lodge—the den of a beaver

rodent—a small mammal with fur and sharp front teeth

symbol—something that stands for something else. People use symbols to show what is important to them.

Read More

Hall, Margaret. *Beavers*. North Mankato, MN: Capstone Press, 2007.

Oldland, Nicholas. *The Busy Beaver* (Life in the Wild). Toronto, ON: Kids Can Press, 2011.

Internet Sites

FactHound offers a safe, fun way to find Internet sites related to this book. All of the sites on FactHound have been researched by our staff.

Here's all you do:

Visit *www.facthound.com*

Type in this code: 9781491470916

Check out projects, games and lots more at
www.capstonekids.com

Index

Word Count: 269
Grade: 1
Early-Intervention Level: 17